At home

En casa

ehn *kah*-sah

Illustrated by Clare Beaton

Ilustraciones de Clare Beaton

b small publishing

door

la puerta

lah poo-*air*tah

window

la ventana

lah ven*tah*-nah

chair

la silla

lah *see*-yah

table

la mesa

lah *meh*-sah

bed

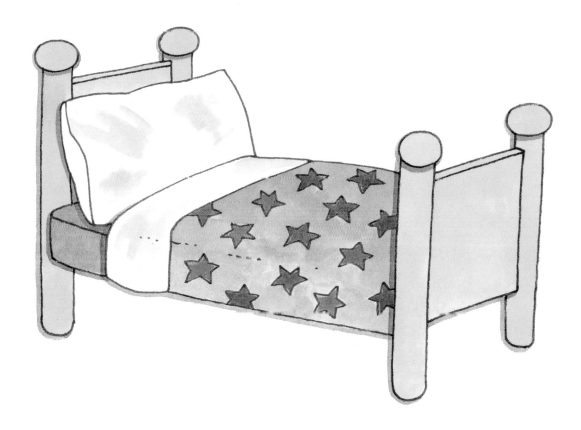

la cama

lah *kamah*

bath

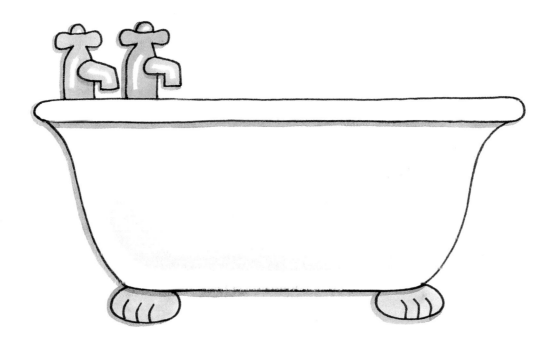

la bañera

lah ban-*yeh*-rah

fridge

el refrigerador

el reh-free-hair-ah-*dohr*

television

el televisor

el tehleh-vee-*sohr*

telephone

el teléfono

el teh*leh*-foh-no

cupboard

el armario

el arm-*ahree*-o

clock

el reloj

el reh-*loh*

A simple guide to pronouncing Spanish words

- Read this guide as naturally as possible, as if it were standard British English.
- Put stress on the letters in *italics*.

En casa	ehn *kah*-sa	**At home**
la puerta	lah poo-*air*tah	**door**
la ventana	lah ven*tah*-nah	**window**
la silla	lah *see*-yah	**chair**
la mesa	lah *meh*-sah	**table**
la cama	lah *kam*ah	**bed**
la bañera	lah ban-*yeh*-rah	**bath**
el refrigerador	el reh-free-hair-ah-*dohr*	**fridge**
el televisor	el tehleh-vee-*sohr*	**television**
el teléfono	el teh*leh*-foh-no	**telephone**
el armario	el arm-*ah*ree-o	**cupboard**
el reloj	el reh-*loh*	**clock**

Published by b small publishing
The Book Shed, 36 Leyborne Park, Kew, Richmond, Surrey, TW9 3HA, UK
www.bsmall.co.uk www.facebook.com/bsmallpublishing twitter.com/bsmallbear
© b small publishing, 2001 and 2012 (new cover)
1 2 3 4 5
All rights reserved.
Printed in China by WKT Company Ltd.
ISBN: 978-1-908164-41-4 (UK paperback)
Cataloguing-in-Publication Data:
A catalogue record for this book is available from the British Library